The Subprime Catastrophe:

Lessons from the 2008 Financial Crisis

The Financial Quill

Copyright 2024 @The Financial Quill

- Chapter 1: Iceland's Dream - A Nation on the Brink of Utopia.......... 3
- Chapter 2: The Banking Frenzy.. 6
- Chapter 3: A Façade of Prosperity... 9
- Chapter 4: Wall Street's Appetite... 13
- Chapter 5: The Dot-Com Delusion... 24
- Chapter 6: The Pandora's Box of Finance... 29
- Chapter 7: Fueling the Inferno... 35
- Chapter 8: The Housing Mirage - A Bubble Built on Debt................ 39
- Chapter 9: Collapse, Bailouts, and the Human Cost........................... 79
- Chapter 10: The Unfinished Revolution... 105

Chapter 1: Iceland's Dream - A Nation on the Brink of Utopia

Iceland is a robust democracy that boasts a high quality of life and, until recently, remarkably low rates of unemployment and government debt. Our nation enjoyed a comprehensive infrastructure befitting a modern society, which included an impressive reliance on clean energy sources, sustainable food production practices, and fisheries carefully managed under a quota system to preserve marine ecosystems.

We also provided quality healthcare accessible to all, coupled with an excellent education system that nurtured the minds of future generations, ensuring that our children were well-equipped for the challenges of tomorrow.

The air was pristine, fostering a healthy environment, while crime remained minimal, contributing to the overall sense of safety and community.

It was truly a wonderful place for families to call home; we were on the verge of achieving the lofty status of "the end of history," a testament to our progress and stability, a dream that many believed we could sustain indefinitely.

However, in 2000, Iceland's government initiated a wide-ranging policy of deregulation that would have catastrophic effects, first on the environment and subsequently on the economy.

This marked the start of a troubling transformation in the nation's approach to its natural resources, as the government began to prioritize corporate interests over the well-being of its citizens.

They started by permitting multinational corporations like Alcoa to construct massive aluminum smelting facilities, which would not only consume vast amounts of energy but also threaten the delicate balance of the local ecosystems.

As these corporations sought to exploit Iceland's abundant geothermal and hydroelectric resources, the consequences became increasingly apparent. Many of the most stunning regions in the highlands, renowned for their vibrant colors and unique geological formations, are geothermal; thus, nothing comes without a price. The pristine landscapes that once attracted tourists and nurtured local communities now stood at risk, signaling a profound shift from sustainability to unchecked industrialization, a transition that left many citizens feeling disillusioned and ignored.

Chapter 2: The Banking Frenzy

Simultaneously, the government undertook the momentous step of privatizing the three largest banks in Iceland, which led to one of the most unrestrained experiments in financial deregulation ever undertaken in modern history.

How could such a catastrophic decision transpire in a nation known for its rugged yet pristine landscapes? Finance surged to the forefront, taking over the economy and essentially devastating the country in just five short years.

These three relatively small banks, which had never before operated beyond Iceland's borders, embarked on a reckless borrowing spree, accumulating a staggering $120 billion—an amount ten times the size of Iceland's entire economy.

In an atmosphere of excess and greed, the bankers lavished money upon themselves, their peers, and their associates, resulting in a colossal economic bubble; stock prices soared to dizzying heights, and property values more than doubled, creating an illusion of prosperity that masked the underlying vulnerabilities of the economy.

Amid this frenzy, Iceland's bubble produced figures like Yan Asare Johanneson, a financier who borrowed billions from the banks to acquire upscale retail ventures in London.

His lavish spending spree didn't stop there; he also indulged in the purchase of a pinstriped private jet, a luxurious $40 million yacht, and an opulent penthouse in Manhattan, all while spinning a narrative of success that benefitted only a select few.

Newspapers frequently splashed headlines about this millionaire acquiring prestigious companies in the UK, Finland, or France, conveniently omitting the fact that he had taken a billion-dollar loan from a local bank to finance those extravagant purchases, thus masking the underlying fragility of the economy and the systemic risks involved.

Chapter 3: A Façade of Prosperity

The banks, in a calculated move to bolster their liquidity, established money market funds and actively encouraged depositors to withdraw their hard-earned savings, enticing them to invest in these seemingly lucrative schemes.

The deposit system, under immense pressure, required every resource it could muster to maintain the façade of stability. Esteemed American accounting firms, including KPMG, conducted thorough audits of the Icelandic banks and investment firms, reporting back with glowing assessments and finding no discrepancies or red flags.

Meanwhile, American credit rating agencies heralded Iceland as an exceptional model of modern banking and financial success.

In a pivotal moment in February 2007, one such agency made the bold decision to upgrade the banks to the highest possible rating, AAA, a move that sent ripples of optimism through the markets, reinforcing the illusion of safety and soundness.

This prestigious rating even extended to the government itself, as officials traveled alongside the bankers, participating in a carefully orchestrated public relations spectacle designed to showcase Iceland's financial prowess to the world, while hiding the growing cracks beneath the surface.

When Iceland's banks collapsed at the end of 2008, the economic fallout was swift and devastating, with unemployment tripling in a mere six months. The impact was felt by every citizen, as many individuals suddenly found themselves stripped of their life savings, their financial futures thrown into chaos.

The very regulators tasked with safeguarding the populace had tragically failed to act, leaving the country vulnerable at a critical moment. Imagine the scene: two lawyers from the regulatory body arrive at one of the banks to discuss a pressing issue, their hearts heavy with the weight of responsibility.

As they pull up, they are greeted by the sight of 19 gleaming SUVs parked outside, an imposing symbol of the bank's power and influence that loomed over the regulators. Stepping inside, they are met by a formidable wall of 19 lawyers, all poised and ready to counter any arguments the regulators might dare to present. I

t is a high-stakes environment where, should they perform exceptionally well in this adversarial setting, the regulators might even receive enticing job offers to join the very institutions they are meant to oversee, a conflict of interest that further complicates their mission.

Alarmingly, one-third of Iceland's financial regulators ultimately transitioned to positions within the banks, a troubling trend that highlights a broader issue of regulatory capture. This phenomenon is not unique to Iceland; similar problems can be observed in the bustling streets of New York, where the lines between regulation and financial interests often blur, creating an environment ripe for exploitation.

Chapter 4: Wall Street's Appetite

What do you think about current Wall Street incomes? Excessive, I've been told. It's extremely challenging for the IMF to criticize the United States. I wouldn't go that far; we deeply regret our violations of US law. They're astonished by how much cocaine Wall Streeters can consume and still manage to show up for work the next day. I wasn't familiar with credit default swaps; I'm a bit old-fashioned. Has Larry Summers ever expressed regret? I don't hear confessions; the government's merely writing checks — that's Plan A, Plan B, and Plan C. Would you support legal restrictions on executive pay? I would not. Are you comfortable with the compensation levels in the financial services sector? If they've earned it, then yes, I am. Do you believe they've earned it? Yes, I think they have.

So, you've aided these individuals in wrecking the world? You could say that; they were reaping enormous private gains at the expense of the public, a stark reminder of the consequences of unregulated greed. When you start believing that something can be created from nothing, it becomes very hard to resist, and the allure of easy wealth can blind even the most prudent. I'm worried that many people wish to revert to the old ways of operating before the crisis, longing for the days of easy profits without consideration for the ramifications. I received numerous anonymous emails from bankers expressing their concerns, saying, "You can't quote me, but I'm really worried." Why do you think there's not a more thorough investigation underway? Because then you'd identify the culprits, and that's a truth many are unwilling to confront. Do you think Columbia Business School has any notable conflicts of interest? I don't see that we do, yet in the intricate web of finance and academia, one must wonder how truly clear those lines are.

The regulators failed to do their jobs; they had the authority to act on every case I presented while serving as State Attorney General, but they simply didn't want to. Over that weekend, Lehman Brothers, one of the most respected and largest investment banks, was compelled to declare bankruptcy, while Merrill Lynch was forced to sell itself in a desperate bid for survival. Today, crisis discussions are ongoing as world financial markets have plummeted following the dramatic events of September 2008. The bankruptcy of Lehman Brothers and the collapse of the world's largest insurance company, AIG, sparked a global financial crisis that reverberated across economies. Markets were gripped overnight, with Asian stock indices plummeting—recording the largest single-day drop in history. Stock prices continued to decline in the aftermath of Lehman's failure, resulting in a global recession that cost the world tens of trillions of dollars, left 30 million people unemployed, and doubled the national debt of the United States. If you assess the costs—the destruction of equity and housing wealth, the loss of jobs and income—15 million people worldwide could fall below the poverty line, a staggering humanitarian crisis that echoes the failures of the financial system.

This is an immensely expansive crisis; it was not an accident but rather the result of an out-of-control industry that had spiraled beyond the limits of oversight. Since the 1980s, the growth of the US financial sector has led to increasingly severe financial crises, each inflicting more damage while the industry amassed greater profits.

After the Great Depression, the United States experienced 40 years of economic growth without a single financial crisis due to strict regulation. Most regular banks were local entities prohibited from speculating with depositor savings, maintaining a protective barrier for consumers. Investment banks, which managed stock and bond trading, were small private partnerships, fostering a culture of accountability and caution.

In the traditional investment banking model, the partners invested their own money and closely supervised its use; they were eager to live comfortably but wary of risking everything, understanding that their fortunes hinged on prudent financial practices.

Paul Volcker served in the Treasury Department and was chairman of the Federal Reserve from 1979 to 1987. Before his government career, he was a financial economist at Chase Manhattan Bank, a position that provided him with valuable insights into the inner workings of the financial sector. When I left Chase to join the Treasury in 1969, my income was around $45,000 a year, a respectable sum in those days. Morgan Stanley, in 1972, had about 110 employees, one office, and $12 million in capital, a far cry from the sprawling financial behemoths we see today.

Now, Morgan Stanley employs 5,000 workers, boasts several billion in capital, and has offices worldwide, reflecting the vast expansion of the financial industry. The financial industry exploded in the 1980s; investment banks went public, granting them vast amounts of shareholder capital and enabling them to take on greater risks without accountability. Individuals on Wall Street began to accumulate wealth at an alarming rate, a phenomenon that would soon lead to reckless behavior. I had a friend who was a bond trader at Merrill Lynch in the 1970s; he worked as a train conductor at night because, with three kids, he couldn't support his family solely on what a bond trader earned. By 1986, he was making millions, believing it was due to his intelligence, yet little did he know that the system was about to implode under the weight of its own excesses.

The foremost priority for the nation was restoring economic prosperity in the wake of the impending crisis.

In 1981, President Ronald Reagan appointed his Treasury Secretary, the CEO of Merrill Lynch, Donald Regan. Wall Street and the president were in sync; I've spoken to many Wall Street leaders, and they all voiced their unwavering support for the president, believing that deregulation would pave the way for unprecedented growth. The Reagan administration, bolstered by economists and financial lobbyists, embarked on a three-decade-long journey of financial deregulation that would fundamentally reshape the landscape. In 1982, the Reagan administration deregulated savings and loan companies, permitting them to engage in risky investments with depositor funds, a decision that would have dire consequences. By the decade's end, hundreds of savings and loan institutions had failed, costing taxpayers $124 billion and robbing many individuals of their life savings. It might be the largest bank heist in our history; numerous savings and loan executives were imprisoned for plundering their companies, their actions emblematic of the greed that had overtaken the industry.

One of the most extreme instances involved Charles Keating. In 1985, when federal regulators began investigating him, Keating hired an economist named Alan Greenspan, a move that would later prove to be a turning point. In a letter to regulators, Greenspan commended Keating's sound business plans and expertise, claiming he saw no risk in allowing Keating to invest his customers' money.

Keating reportedly paid Greenspan $4,000, a small price for the assurances he sought. Shortly thereafter, Charles Keating was imprisoned for his role in the scandal.

As for Alan Greenspan, President Reagan appointed him chairman of the Federal Reserve, and he was reappointed by Presidents Clinton and George W. Bush, a testament to his influence.

During the Clinton administration, deregulation persisted under Greenspan, Treasury Secretary Robert Rubin, the former CEO of Goldman Sachs, and Larry Summers, a Harvard economics professor who would later face scrutiny for his decisions.

The financial sector, Wall Street, gained power, wielded significant lobbying influence, and gradually captured the political system on both the Democratic and Republican sides, embedding itself in the very fabric of governance.

By the late 1990s, the financial sector had consolidated into a few massive firms, each so large that their failure could jeopardize the entire system.

The Clinton administration facilitated their expansion further, with little concern for the potential fallout. In 1998, Citicorp and Travelers merged to create Citigroup, the largest financial services company globally, a merger that would set a dangerous precedent.

This merger violated the Glass-Steagall Act, a law enacted after the Great Depression that prohibited banks with consumer deposits from engaging in risky investment banking activities, a protective measure designed to safeguard the economy. Acquiring Travelers was illegal, yet Greenspan remained silent, an emblem of the complicity that characterized the era.

The Federal Reserve granted them an exemption for a year, and then, at the urging of Summers and Rubin, Congress passed the Gramm-Leach-Bliley Act, informally known as the Citigroup Relief Act, which overturned Glass-Steagall and paved the way for future mergers, a decision that would have catastrophic consequences.

Why do we have large banks? Because they enjoy monopolistic power, they appreciate lobbying influence, and they know that when they're too big, they'll receive a bailout, thus insulating them from the repercussions of their actions. Markets are inherently unstable, or at least potentially unstable, a reality that regulators often overlook. An appropriate metaphor is oil tankers; they're enormous, requiring compartments to prevent the sloshing oil from capsizing the vessel. The vessel's design must account for this, and after the Depression, regulations introduced watertight compartments to safeguard against disaster. Deregulation has led to the dismantling of compartmentalization, leaving the financial system vulnerable to shocks.

Chapter 5: The Dot-Com Delusion

The next crisis emerged at the end of the 1990s when investment banks fueled a significant bubble in internet stocks, followed by a crash in 2001 that resulted in $5 trillion in investment losses, a staggering figure that reverberated throughout the economy.

The Securities and Exchange Commission, the federal agency established during the Depression to regulate investment banking, remained inactive during this tumultuous period. In the absence of meaningful federal action, and due to the clear failure of self-regulation, it became essential for others to intervene and implement necessary protections.

Elliot Spitzer's investigation uncovered that investment banks had promoted internet companies they knew would fail, a blatant disregard for their fiduciary responsibilities. Stock analysts were compensated based on the volume of business they generated, and their public statements often contradicted private opinions, creating a culture of deceit. Infospace received the highest rating, while an analyst dismissed it as worthless; Excite was also highly rated but labeled "a piece of junk." The defense offered by many investment banks was, "You're wrong; everyone is doing it, and they're well aware of what's happening, so no one should trust these analysts," a deflection that exemplified the pervasive moral hazard.

In December 2002, ten investment banks settled the case for a total of $1.4 billion and pledged to change their practices, though many remained skeptical about their commitment to reform.

Scott Talbot serves as the chief lobbyist for the Financial Services Roundtable, one of Washington's most influential groups, representing nearly all of the world's largest financial firms. Are you comfortable with the fact that several of your member companies have been involved in significant criminal activities? You'll need to be more specific. First of all, criminal activity should not be tolerated, yet the evidence suggests otherwise. Since the onset of deregulation, the world's largest financial firms have repeatedly faced allegations of money laundering, defrauding customers, and falsifying their financial records. Credit Suisse was implicated in funneling money for Iran's nuclear program and its aerospace industry, which manufactures ballistic missiles. Any information that might identify it as Iranian was concealed, reflecting a troubling disregard for international norms. The bank was fined $536 million, a mere slap on the wrist for such egregious behavior. Citibank assisted in transferring $100 million of drug money from Mexico, and did you comment that she should "lose any documents connected with the account"? I mentioned that jokingly; it was early in the investigation, and I didn't mean it seriously, yet it underscores the casual attitude towards serious wrongdoing.

Between 1998 and 2003, Fannie Mae overstated its earnings by over $10 billion, a staggering amount that revealed the depths of deception within the system.

These accounting standards are complex and often subject to expert disagreements, creating an environment ripe for manipulation. CEO Franklin Raines, who previously served as President Clinton's budget director, received more than $52 million in bonuses, a grotesque reward for misconduct.

When UBS was caught aiding wealthy Americans in evading taxes, they refused to cooperate with the US government, further demonstrating the contempt for accountability that pervades the industry. Would you be willing to disclose names if a treaty framework existed?

No, there's no treaty framework. You've acknowledged that you participated in a fraud.

However, while these companies face unprecedented fines, the investment firms are not required to admit any wrongdoing, leaving the public to grapple with the fallout. When you're this large and dealing with so many products and customers, mistakes can happen, but the pattern of behavior suggests a deeper issue. The financial services industry seems to exhibit a level of criminality that is somewhat distinct; when was the last time Cisco, Intel, Google, Apple, or IBM faced such issues? I completely agree with you regarding the contrast between high-tech and financial services, yet the implications of this disparity must not be overlooked.

High-tech is fundamentally a creative sector, where value generation and income come from creating something new and different.

Chapter 6: The Pandora's Box of Finance

Beginning in the 1990s, deregulation and technological advancements led to an explosion of complex financial products known as derivatives.

Economists and bankers claimed they made markets safer, but in reality, they rendered them unstable, a ticking time bomb waiting to explode.

Following the end of the Cold War, many former physicists and mathematicians shifted their skills from Cold War technology to financial markets, collaborating with investment bankers and hedge funds to create new financial instruments that were often poorly understood.

As Warren Buffett remarked, these are "weapons of mass destruction," and their proliferation posed a significant threat to the financial system.

Regulators, politicians, and business leaders failed to recognize the peril posed by financial innovation on the stability of the financial system, blinded by the allure of quick profits.

Using derivatives, bankers could gamble on nearly anything—betting on fluctuations in oil prices, corporate bankruptcies, or even the weather, creating a complex web of risk that was impossible to manage. By the late 1990s, derivatives represented a $50 trillion unregulated market, a staggering sum that dwarfed the size of the underlying assets.

In 1998, an attempt was made to regulate them, a move that would prove to be both controversial and consequential. Brooksley Bourne, who graduated at the top of her class from Stanford Law School and was the first woman to edit a major law review, had previously run the derivatives practice at Arnold and Porter. Appointed by President Clinton to chair the Commodity Futures Trading Commission, overseeing the derivatives market, Bourne recognized the potential destabilizing nature of this market and felt compelled to act.

In May 1998, the CFTC proposed regulating derivatives, a proposal that was met with immediate resistance from powerful interests. The response from Clinton's Treasury Department was swift and hostile. I happened to enter Brooksley's office just as she hung up the phone, and the blood had drained from her face. She looked at me and said, "That was Larry Summers; he had 13 bankers in his office." She conveyed it in a very intimidating manner, essentially directing her to halt her efforts, a moment that encapsulated the battle between regulation and unchecked ambition.

The banks had become heavily reliant on these activities for their earnings, leading to a monumental struggle to prevent this set of instruments from being regulated. Following Summers' phone call, Greenspan, Rubin, and SEC Chairman Arthur Levitt issued a joint statement denouncing Bourne and advocating for legislation to keep derivatives unregulated, arguing that regulating privately negotiated derivatives transactions by professionals was unnecessary.

Unfortunately, she was overruled, first by the Clinton administration and subsequently by Congress, a decision that would have far-reaching consequences. In 2000, Senator Phil Gramm played a significant role in passing a bill that essentially exempted derivatives from regulation, a move that would lay the groundwork for future financial calamities.

They claimed that such regulation would unify markets and reduce regulatory burdens, a justification that masked the dangerous implications of their actions. I believe we need to pursue this. We genuinely hope to advance legislation this year that appropriately establishes legal certainty for over-the-counter derivatives. I fully support Secretary Summers' remarks, yet the rhetoric belied the reality of the situation.

In December 2000, Congress enacted the Commodity Futures Modernization Act, crafted with assistance from financial industry lobbyists, a bill that effectively prohibited the regulation of derivatives. Once that was accomplished, the use of derivatives and financial innovation surged dramatically, unchecked and unbridled.

By the time George W. Bush assumed office in 2001, the US financial sector had become far more profitable, concentrated, and powerful than ever before.

Dominating this industry were five investment banks, two financial conglomerates, three securities insurance companies, and three rating agencies, a concentration of power that would prove disastrous. Linking them all together was the securitization food chain—a new system that connected trillions of dollars in mortgages and other loans with investors worldwide, creating a complex network that obscured risk.

Chapter 7: Fueling the Inferno

Thirty years ago, when seeking a home loan, the lender expected you to repay it.

You would receive a loan from a lender who wanted you to pay them back; this system has since evolved into securitization, where those who issue the loans are no longer at risk if repayment fails, a fundamental shift that undermines accountability. In the old system, when a homeowner consistently paid their mortgage, the money went directly to their local lender. Since mortgages took decades to repay, lenders were cautious, a practice that has all but vanished in the new model.

In the new system, lenders sold the mortgages to investment banks, which then bundled thousands of mortgages along with other loans—such as car loans, student loans, and credit card debts—to create complex derivatives known as collateralized debt obligations (CDOs).

The investment banks subsequently sold these CDOs to investors, enticing them with the promise of high returns.

Now, when homeowners made their mortgage payments, the money flowed to investors worldwide, creating a disconnect between lenders and borrowers that would ultimately lead to disaster. The investment banks compensated rating agencies to assess the CDOs, and many received AAA ratings—the highest possible investment grade—an endorsement that belied the underlying risks.

This made CDOs attractive to retirement funds, which were restricted to purchasing highly rated securities, yet the system was a ticking time bomb; lenders became indifferent to whether a borrower had the ability to repay, leading to increasingly risky loans.

Investment banks were equally unconcerned; the more CDOs they sold, the greater their profits, and the rating agencies, being compensated by the investment banks, bore no liability for erroneous ratings, a dangerous arrangement that went unchecked for far too long. There were no regulatory constraints, providing a green light to indiscriminately issue more and more loans, a recipe for disaster.

Between 2000 and 2003, the volume of mortgage loans made each year nearly quadrupled, a staggering increase that illustrated the rampant speculation within the market.

Everyone involved in this securitization food chain, from start to finish, prioritized volume over the quality of the mortgages, focusing on maximizing fees, a practice that would have dire consequences. In the early 2000s, there was a significant rise in the riskiest loans, known as subprime loans, a category that would soon become synonymous with the coming crisis.

However, when thousands of these subprime loans were bundled into CDOs, many still received AAA ratings, a glaring oversight that reflected the failures of the system. It would have been feasible to create derivative products that mitigated these risks—products with equivalent deductibles and limits on the risks involved—but they failed to do so. In hindsight, they should have made those adjustments, yet the allure of easy profits proved too tempting to resist. Were they aware they were engaging in dangerous practices? I think they were, as all the incentives offered to mortgage brokers by financial institutions were centered around selling the most lucrative products, which were often predatory loans. If a banker could earn more by placing you in a subprime loan, that's exactly where they would direct you, a clear conflict of interest that went unaddressed.

Chapter 8: The Housing Mirage - A Bubble Built on Debt

Suddenly, hundreds of billions of dollars began to pour through the securitization pipeline, resulting in soaring home purchases and escalating housing prices, as virtually anyone could qualify for a mortgage, regardless of their financial situation. The financial bubble in real estate history is undeniably evident; people can see, live in, and rent out their assets. There was an immense housing boom that defied logic, driven by the financial sector's appetite for financing. The last housing bubble occurred in the late 1980s, where the rise in home prices was comparatively modest. That bubble resulted in a notably severe recession. From 1996 to 2006, real home prices virtually doubled, creating an unsustainable situation.

At $500 a ticket, people came to learn how to obtain their own slice of the American dream. Major firms like Goldman Sachs, Bear Stearns, Lehman Brothers, and Merrill Lynch were fully invested in this market, their interests intertwined with the very fabric of the economy. Subprime lending alone surged from $30 billion in annual funding to over $600 billion within a decade, a staggering increase that illustrated the rampant speculation and disregard for risk. They were aware of the unfolding situation, yet continued their reckless practices, driven by the desire for profits. Countrywide Financial, the largest subprime lender, issued $97 billion in loans, reaping over $1 billion in profits as a result, a stark indicator of the perverse incentives at play.

On Wall Street, annual cash bonuses soared, creating immense wealth for traders and CEOs during the bubble, a phenomenon that would soon lead to widespread discontent.

Lehman Brothers was a leading underwriter of subprime loans, with CEO Richard Fuld taking home $485 million, a staggering sum that underscored the disconnect between executive compensation and performance.

This housing and credit bubble generated profits amounting to hundreds of billions of dollars, yet these profits were illusory, merely money fabricated by the system and recorded as income. Two to three years later, when defaults occurred, it would all be erased, leaving devastation in its wake.

In hindsight, it was a colossal national—if not global—Ponzi scheme, a reality that many were unwilling to confront. The Federal Reserve board had extensive authority to regulate the mortgage sector through the Home Ownership and Equity Protection Act, yet Fed Chairman Alan Greenspan declined to exercise it, citing ideological beliefs against regulation.

For two decades, Robert GDA led Greenlining, a formidable consumer advocacy group, and met regularly with Greenspan, attempting to raise awareness. He presented examples from Countrywide and 150 different complex adjustable-rate mortgages, arguing that even someone with a doctorate in mathematics would struggle to understand them well enough to know which options were beneficial. Initially, it seemed Greenspan might take action, but as discussions progressed, it became apparent he was entrenched in his ideology, a stubbornness that would have dire consequences.

In 2005, during our biannual meetings with him, he remained steadfast. In this remarkable age of instant global communication, the rapid and efficient movement of capital contributed to unprecedented prosperity, yet also to systemic vulnerabilities.

The SEC saw a significant reduction in its enforcement division, which you also affirmed, correct?

Yes, I believe there has been a systematic dismantling of the agency's capabilities due to staff cuts. The SEC's Office of Risk Management was reduced to a staff of one. When that individual went home at night, he could turn off the lights — the metaphorical lights that had dimmed on regulatory oversight.

During the bubble, investment banks borrowed extensively to acquire more loans and create more CDOs, a practice that would soon prove disastrous. The ratio of borrowed funds to the bank's own capital was termed leverage, a critical measure of risk. The greater the borrowing, the higher the leverage, a situation that created a precarious balance. In 2004, Henry Paulson, CEO of Goldman Sachs, lobbied the SEC to ease leverage limits, enabling banks to substantially boost their borrowing in a reckless manner. The SEC inexplicably permitted investment banks to gamble more; it was madness, and the consequences would soon unfold.

These institutions were, without a doubt, among the most sophisticated financial entities. They dominated derivative activities in the U.S. We consulted with them regarding their comfort levels, and they believed the numbers were appropriate, a troubling indication of the prevailing culture of complacency. The commissioner voted in favor of adopting the rule amendments and new regulations as the staff had recommended, correct? Yes, indeed, it was unanimous, a decision that would have catastrophic implications. The degree of leverage in the financial system became terrifying, with investment banks leveraging as high as 33:1 — meaning a mere 3% drop in their asset base could render them insolvent, a precarious situation that invited disaster.

Another looming threat within the financial system was AIG, the world's largest insurance company, which was selling vast amounts of derivatives known as credit default swaps to investors holding CDOs.

These swaps functioned like an insurance policy; an investor who bought one paid AIG a quarterly premium, and in the event of a CDO failure, AIG would compensate for the losses, yet the underlying risks were poorly understood. However, unlike traditional insurance, speculators could also acquire credit default swaps from AIG to bet against CDOs they didn't own. In insurance, you can only insure something you possess; for instance, I can insure my house. The derivatives landscape allowed anyone to insure a house, meaning multiple parties could insure it, leading to inflated losses if that house burned down, a scenario that exemplified the perils of the unregulated financial environment.

Since credit default swaps were unregulated, AIG had no obligation to set aside funds for potential losses, a reckless approach that would soon backfire.

Instead, AIG rewarded its employees with hefty cash bonuses as soon as contracts were finalized, a practice that incentivized short-term thinking. If the CDOs later failed, AIG would bear the consequences, a dire reality that few anticipated. People were essentially incentivized to take enormous risks during prosperous times to yield short-term revenues and bonuses, which ultimately would drive the firm to bankruptcy — a wholly distorted compensation system that favored immediate gains over long-term stability.

AIG's financial products division in London issued credit default swaps worth $500 billion during the bubble, many tied to CDOs supported by subprime mortgages, a staggering amount that illustrated the scale of the operation.

The 400 employees at AIG FP earned $3.5 billion between 2000 and 2007, a sum that underscored the disconnect between risk and reward. Joseph Cassano, head of AIG FP, personally made $315 million, a fortune built on a foundation of risk that few understood. It's hard for us, without being flippant, to envision any scenario within reason where we'd lose even $1 on those transactions, a statement that now rings hollow in the wake of the crisis.

In 2007, AIG's auditors raised alarms; one, Joseph St. Dennis, resigned in protest after Cassano repeatedly blocked his attempts to investigate AIG FP's accounting. Let me mention one individual who didn't receive a bonus while others did: St. Dennis, who tried to warn you about the significant issues you were facing, ultimately quit in frustration and received no bonus, a sobering reminder of the culture of silence that prevailed.

In 2005, Raghuram Rajan, then chief economist of the International Monetary Fund, presented a paper at the annual Jackson Hole Symposium, the premier banking conference globally.

The audience included central bankers from around the world, including Greenspan, Ben Bernanke, and Larry Summers, a gathering of the financial elite. The paper's title essentially questioned whether financial development was making the world riskier, concluding that it indeed was. Rajan's paper examined incentive structures that rewarded massive cash bonuses for short-term profits without imposing penalties for future losses. He argued these incentives prompted bankers to take risks that could ultimately jeopardize their firms or even the entire financial system, a warning that went largely unheeded.

It's easy to generate performance by increasing risk, so it's crucial to compensate for risk-adjusted performance, which is where the real problems lie. Rajan hit the nail on the head when he stated that while you claimed to have found a way to generate higher profits with less risk, the reality was you had discovered a method to increase profits with more risk—a significant distinction that many failed to grasp. Summers was vocally critical, perceiving me as denouncing the financial world's transformation and expressing concern over regulations that might reverse this entire shift, essentially accusing me of being a liar, a defense mechanism that reflected the denial rampant in the industry.

If you could earn an additional $2 million or $10 million a year by putting your financial institution at risk, while someone else bore the cost, would you take that gamble?

Most Wall Street professionals would say yes, a troubling indictment of the prevailing ethos. It was never enough; they didn't want just one home; they desired five homes, a lavish penthouse on Park Avenue, and their own private jet, a lifestyle that epitomized excess and greed.

Do you think this industry justifies such extremely high compensation levels? I would take issue with your term "very high." It's all relative; you might have a $14 million oceanfront home in Florida, a summer getaway in Sun Valley, Idaho, and a couple with an art collection filled with million-dollar paintings.

Richard Fuld never appeared on the trading floor, opting for art advisors who were frequently present instead, a stark reminder of the disconnect between the executives and the realities of the workers. He had his own private elevator, designed to minimize contact with others, requiring technicians to program it for his driver's calls in the morning, while a security guard would hold the elevator, a subtle indicator of the privilege that had become commonplace among the elite.

There was only a two or three-second window for him to interact with people before he would hop in and head straight to his office, a routine that underscored his isolation from the very system he had helped to create.

Lehman Brothers owned several corporate jets, correct?

Yes, there were six, including 767s, and they also had a helicopter, a luxury that seemed excessive for a firm that was purportedly in financial trouble. Isn't that an excessive number of aircraft for an individual? Well, we're dealing with Type A personalities, and such competitive behavior is common in the banking industry, becoming a sort of pissing contest — my jet is bigger than yours. All the executives were men, and $50 billion deals were deemed too small, so they aimed for hundred-billion-dollar transactions, a mindset that prioritized size over substance. These individuals are risk-takers and impulsive; it's ingrained in their personalities, and it extends beyond their professional lives. It's not unusual for them to frequent strip clubs and use drugs; there's a noticeable prevalence of cocaine use and prostitution, a lifestyle that reflects the moral decay at the heart of the industry.

Recent neuroscience studies have shown that when individuals earn money in a game, the same part of the brain stimulated by cocaine lights up, a frightening parallel between financial gain and addiction. Many believe they must engage in such behaviors to gain promotions or recognition; the drive for success often leads to self-destructive choices. According to a Bloomberg article, business entertainment accounts for 5% of revenue for New York derivatives brokers, often involving strip clubs, prostitution, and drugs, a reality that few are willing to confront. One New York broker filed a lawsuit in 2007 against his firm, alleging he was required to hire prostitutes to entertain traders, highlighting the unethical practices that had become normalized.

There's a blatant disregard for the societal impact of their actions; they have no qualms about using a prostitute and then returning home to their wives, a stark demonstration of the ethical bankruptcy that permeated the culture. How many clients did you have at that time? Approximately 10,000, a staggering number that illustrates the scale of the operations. What percentage were from Wall Street? Among the high-end clients, probably 40 to 50%. Were all the major Wall Street firms represented there? Yes, Goldman Sachs, Lehman Brothers — they were all involved. Morgan Stanley was a little less so, but Goldman was quite prominent. Many clients would call me asking if I could arrange a Lamborghini for the night for a girl, a request that reflects the entitlement and excess that characterized the elite. These men were spending corporate funds, often charging services to computer repair, trading research, or consulting for market compliance, a blatant abuse of resources. They typically just provided a piece of letterhead for their invoices, a thin veneer of legitimacy that concealed the underlying exploitation.

You believe this pattern of behavior extends to the senior management of the firms? Absolutely, I know for a fact it does; it reaches the very top, a troubling reality that speaks to the culture of complicity.

A friend of mine, involved in a significant financial firm, remarked that it was about time I understood subprime mortgages, a statement that encapsulated the arrogance of the industry. He arranged a meeting with his trading desk, and the tech guy got excited, quickly pulling up a Goldman Sachs issue that was a complete disaster.

Borrowers had, on average, financed 99.3% of their home prices, meaning they had no equity, a situation that was unsustainable. If anything went awry, they would walk away from the mortgage; this was not a sensible loan. Yet somehow, 8,000 of these loans were structured, and by the time Goldman Sachs and the rating agencies were done, two-thirds received AAA ratings, equating them to government securities in terms of safety—a glaring oversight that would soon come to haunt the system. It was utterly insane, yet few were willing to challenge the status quo.

Goldman Sachs sold at least $3.1 billion worth of these toxic CDOs in the first half of 2006, a staggering amount that illustrated the scale of the operation. At that time, Henry Paulson was the CEO of Goldman Sachs and the highest-paid CEO on Wall Street, a position that afforded him significant influence. "Good morning, welcome to the White House.

I'm pleased to announce that I will nominate Henry Paulson as Secretary of the Treasury. He has a lifetime of business experience and an intimate knowledge of financial markets, earning a reputation for candor and integrity." You might think it would be challenging for Paulson to adjust to a modest government salary, but taking the treasury secretary role was the best financial decision of his life.

Paulson had to divest his $485 million in Goldman stock when he took the government position, but due to a law enacted by the first President Bush, he didn't owe any taxes on it, saving him $50 million, a windfall that few could have anticipated.

By October 2007, a third of the mortgages had already defaulted, a staggering statistic that illustrated the depth of the crisis. One group that had invested in these now worthless securities was the Public Employees Retirement System of Mississippi, which provides monthly benefits to over 880,000 retirees, a sobering reminder of the human cost of the financial collapse.

They lost millions and are now suing Goldman Sachs, a desperate attempt to reclaim what was lost in the wake of the crisis. By late 2006, Goldman took things a step further; it didn't merely sell toxic CDOs but began actively betting against them while assuring customers they were high-quality investments, a brazen act of betrayal that revealed the depths of corporate malfeasance.

By purchasing credit default swaps from AIG, Goldman could bet against CDOs it didn't own and profit when they failed, a practice that highlighted the moral hazard at play.

I inquired whether anyone informed customers that they no longer endorsed those mortgages. They didn't explicitly say anything, but you could sense the laughter coming through the phone, a chilling reminder of the callousness that characterized the industry.

Goldman Sachs acquired at least $20 billion in credit default swaps from AIG, realizing that AIG itself might collapse, prompting them to spend $150 million insuring against AIG's potential downfall, a move that underscored the depths of their self-interest. Then, in 2007, Goldman went even further, creating CDOs that were specifically structured so that the more money their customers lost, the more profits Goldman Sachs made, a grotesque manipulation of the system.

You sold $600 million of Timberwolf Securities, correct? Before you sold them, what did your sales team communicate among themselves? "Boy, Timberwolf was one lousy deal," was an email I received in late June, a candid admission that belied the prevailing narrative. You sold Timberwolf after that, right? Yes, we executed trades afterward. The next email, dated July 2007, instructed the sales force that Timberwolf should be their top priority to sell, despite its poor reputation, a clear indication of the disconnect between risk and responsibility. If you have an adverse interest to your client, you are obligated to disclose that to them. That's my question. Yes, Mr. Chairman, I'm trying to grasp this. I believe you understand, but I don't think you want to answer. Do you think you have a duty to act in your clients' best interests?

Again, Senator, I must reiterate that we have a duty to serve our clients by providing prices on transactions that they request. How do you feel about selling securities that your own team deems worthless? I believe they would, again in a hypothetical scenario... No, this is not hypothetical; this is real. Well, I haven't heard anything today that leads me to believe something went amiss. Isn't there a conflict when you sell something to someone while simultaneously betting against that same security without disclosing this to the buyer? In the context of market-making, I don't view that as a conflict, a troubling assertion that reflects the prevailing mindset within the industry. When you learned your employees referred to Timberwolf as a lousy deal, how did you feel? I find it very unfortunate that those words were exchanged via email, a reflection of the moral decay that had infiltrated the culture.

It is unfortunate, but I don't email; how about feeling that way? I think it's regrettable for anyone to express that sentiment in any form, yet the reality is stark. Is it your understanding that your competitors were engaging in similar activities? Yes, and in many instances, to a greater degree than us, a haunting admission that underscores the systemic nature of the crisis. Hedge fund manager John Paulson earned $2 billion betting against the mortgage market, a staggering sum that illustrated the depths of the exploitation. When Paulson exhausted available mortgage securities to short, he collaborated with Goldman Sachs and Deutsche Bank to create more, a blatant manipulation of the system. Morgan Stanley also sold mortgage securities while simultaneously betting against them, and is now facing a lawsuit from the government employees' retirement fund of the Virgin Islands for fraud, a troubling indication of the pervasive corruption.

You might think pension funds would question the rationale behind purchasing subprime securities. Yet, they relied on Moody's and Standard & Poor's, who assured them these were AAA-rated, a blind faith that would soon prove disastrous. None of these securities were issued without the premature approval of the rating agencies, a reality that illustrates the systemic failures at play. The three major rating agencies—Moody's, S&P, and Fitch—earned billions by granting high ratings to risky securities, a perverse incentive that led to widespread malpractice. Moody's, the largest rating agency, saw its profits quadruple from 2000 to 2007, a staggering figure that highlighted the disconnect between risk and reward. Moody's and S&P were compensated based on the frequency of their ratings reports; the more structured securities they rated AAA, the higher their earnings for the quarter, a system fundamentally at odds with the principles of sound financial oversight.

Imagine if you approached the New York Times, proposing, "If you write a positive article, I'll pay you $500,000, but if you don't, I'll pay nothing." The rating agencies could have halted the party, stating they would tighten their standards and immediately cut off much funding to risky borrowers. AAA-rated instruments exploded from a few to thousands, with hundreds of billions of dollars being rated annually, a staggering increase that masked the underlying risks. I've now testified before both houses of Congress regarding the credit rating agency issue, and on both occasions, they brought out prominent First Amendment lawyers, arguing that when they rate something as AAA, it's merely their opinion, which shouldn't be relied upon. S&P's ratings express their opinions—they are just opinions, yet those opinions had devastating consequences for countless individuals.

We've had numerous economists on our programs warning that this is a bubble poised to burst, potentially leading to significant economic issues. What is the worst-case scenario if housing prices plummet nationwide? Well, I don't accept your premise; such a situation seems highly unlikely. We've never witnessed a nationwide decline in house prices, a statement that now seems naïve in hindsight. Ben Bernanke became the Federal Reserve Board chair in February 2006, coinciding with the peak of subprime lending, yet despite numerous warnings, Bernanke and the Federal Reserve took no action, a critical misstep that would soon be felt across the economy.

Robert GDA met with Bernanke and the Federal Reserve board three times after Bernanke took office. Only during the final meeting did he suggest that a problem existed and that the government should investigate, a glaring oversight that underscored the systemic failures at play.

When did this meeting occur? In 2009, March 11, in Washington, D.C. This year? Yes, this year. So, during the preceding two years, you met with him, even in 2008? Yes, one of the six Federal Reserve board governors under Bernanke was Frederick Mishkin, appointed by President Bush in 2006. Did you attend the semiannual meetings held by Robert GDA and Greenlining with the Federal Reserve board? Yes, I participated in the Consumer Community Affairs committee.

He explicitly warned about the ongoing issues, bringing loan documentation that illustrated the types of loans frequently issued. He was listened to cordially, yet nothing was executed, a sobering reminder of the complacency that characterized the response.

I'm uncertain about the specifics of the information he provided; to be honest, I can't recall such discussions. However, issues were indeed arising, but the question became how pervasive they were. Why didn't you investigate further? I believe people did look into it; we had a dedicated group examining the situation. For whatever reason, you can't be serious. If you had investigated, you would have uncovered significant issues, yet the inertia of the system proved insurmountable.

As early as 2004, the FBI had already begun warning about a mortgage fraud epidemic, reporting inflated appraisals, falsified loan documents, and other fraudulent practices, a warning that went largely unheeded.

In 2005, the IMF's chief economist Raghuram Rajan cautioned about dangerous incentives that could lead to a crisis, yet his warnings fell on deaf ears. Following him were warnings from Nouriel Roubini in 2006, Alan Sloan's articles in Fortune Magazine, and the Washington Post in 2007, along with repeated alerts from the IMF, yet the industry refused to acknowledge the impending disaster. I represent the institution, and I can assure you that the crisis confronting us is immense, a reality that must not be ignored. Who did you consult? Treasury officials, among others, yet their complacency was equally troubling.

In May 2007, hedge fund manager Bill Ackman circulated a presentation titled "Who's Holding the Bag?" detailing how the bubble would burst, a forewarning that few took seriously.

In early 2008, Charles Morris published his book about the looming crisis, yet the industry continued to operate as if nothing were amiss. It's difficult to ascertain what actions to take; you might suspect that underwriting standards are deteriorating, but you question whether you should intervene, a paralysis that reflects the systemic failures at play. By 2008, home foreclosures skyrocketed, leading to the collapse of the securitization chain, a tragic consequence of unchecked greed. Lenders could no longer offload loans to investment banks, resulting in the failure of numerous lenders, a reality that few could have anticipated.

Chuck Prince of Citigroup famously remarked that they had to "dance until the music stopped," but the music had already halted when he made that statement, a shocking admission that underscored the disconnection from reality.

The market for CDOs collapsed, leaving investment banks holding hundreds of billions in unsellable loans, CDOs, and real estate, a situation that would soon spiral out of control. When the crisis initiated, both the Bush Administration and the Federal Reserve were entirely unprepared, failing to grasp the extent of the situation. At what point did you first think, "This is dangerous; this is serious"? I remember distinctly; one instance was during a G7 meeting in February 2008, where I discussed the issue with Hank Paulson. I vividly recall telling him we were observing a tsunami on the horizon, yet he merely suggested we consider what swimming attire to wear.

What was his reaction? He felt everything was under control. Yes, they were monitoring the situation closely and believed it was manageable—if things are growing, you're not in a recession, right?

We all recognize that. Within days, one of Wall Street's pillars, Bear Stearns, ran out of cash in March 2008 and was acquired for $2 a share by JPMorgan Chase, backed by $30 billion in emergency guarantees from the Federal Reserve, a desperate measure that underscored the fragility of the system.

That was the moment when the administration could have introduced various measures to reduce systemic risk. The information I received from certain entities suggested that the worst was not yet over, that there were more troubles ahead. I observed those investment banks collaborating with the Fed and the SEC to strengthen their liquidity and capital positions, yet the warnings went unheeded. I receive continuous reports; our regulators are quite vigilant, yet the systemic issues remained unaddressed.

On September 7, 2008, Henry Paulson announced the federal takeover of Fannie Mae and Freddie Mac, two colossal mortgage lenders on the verge of collapse. "Nothing about our actions today reflects a changed perspective on the housing correction or the robustness of other U.S. financial institutions." Two days later, Lehman Brothers reported record losses of $3.2 billion, leading to a stock collapse that would send shockwaves through the global economy. The repercussions of Lehman and AIG in September were still shocking, even after the Fannie and Freddie interventions, a stark reminder of the gravity of the situation.

Clearly, there were significant issues in September that no one was aware of. I think that's fair to say. Bear Stearns held an AAA rating just a month before its bankruptcy—more likely it was A2, which was still not considered bankrupt.

No, A2 is still a high investment-grade rating, a troubling contradiction. Lehman Brothers had an A2 rating just days before its failure, and AIG was similarly rated shortly before its bailout. Fannie Mae and Freddie Mac also had AAA ratings when they were rescued, and Citigroup and Merrill Lynch had investment-grade ratings as well. How can that be?

Well, that's a valid question. At no point did the administration approach major institutions to inquire about their positions and assess the seriousness of the situation. No, that's the role of the regulators; they are supposed to comprehend the exposure across various institutions, yet their oversight proved inadequate. They possessed a refined understanding that, I believe, became more nuanced as the crisis unfolded, yet their actions failed to reflect the gravity of the situation.

Forgive me, but that's evidently false. Were you aware in August 2008 of the credit ratings assigned to Lehman Brothers, Merrill Lynch, and AIG, and did you find them accurate? By that time, it was evident that prior ratings had been inaccurate as they had been substantially downgraded. No, there hadn't been downgrades across the board. There was some downgrading in response to industry concerns, but many firms retained A2 ratings until just days before their rescue, a troubling oversight that illustrated the systemic failures at play.

Well, then, my response is that I simply lack sufficient information to confidently address your question regarding this matter.

Governor Mishkin is resigning effective August 31, planning to return to his teaching position at Columbia's Graduate School of Business.

Why did you depart from the Federal Reserve in August 2008, in the midst of the worst financial crisis? I had to revise a textbook, a task that now seems trivial in the context of the unfolding events. His exit leaves the Fed board with three out of seven seats vacant, just when the economy requires it most. I'm sure your textbook is significant and widely read, but in August 2008, isn't it true that more pressing issues were unfolding globally, a reality that must not be ignored?

By Friday, September 12, Lehman Brothers had exhausted its cash reserves, and the entire investment banking sector was rapidly sinking, a situation that demanded urgent action. The stability of the global financial system was at risk. That weekend, Henry Paulson and Timothy Geithner, president of the New York Federal Reserve, convened an emergency meeting with the CEOs of major banks to devise a rescue plan for Lehman, yet the urgency of the situation was palpable.

Lehman wasn't alone; Merrill Lynch, another significant investment bank, was also teetering on the edge of failure. That Sunday, it was acquired by Bank of America, the only bank willing to purchase Lehman, which was Barclays, but British regulators insisted on a financial guarantee from the U.S. government. Paulson declined, a decision that would have catastrophic implications.

We all jumped into a yellow cab and headed to the Federal Reserve Bank, pushing for the bankruptcy proceedings to begin before midnight on September 14. We emphasized that this would be a disastrous event, and at one point, I used the term "Armageddon," stressing the extraordinary market consequences of their proposed actions. You said this? Yes, they acknowledged our concerns but remained convinced that for market stability and progress, Lehman needed to file for bankruptcy, a decision that would soon prove disastrous.

They aimed to calm the markets? Yes, yet the reality was that the markets were anything but calm. When were you first informed that Lehman was, in fact, going to declare bankruptcy? After the fact, a troubling indication of the disconnect between decision-makers and the unfolding crisis. Wow. What was your reaction upon learning this? Holy cow. Paulson and Bernanke had not consulted with other governments and failed to grasp the implications of foreign bankruptcy laws. Lehman Brothers' London office continued operating under British law, which required an immediate shutdown of their office, halting all transactions and leaving thousands of transactions frozen, a situation that reverberated throughout the global economy.

The hedge funds that had assets with Lehman in London discovered, to their utter dismay, that they could not retrieve those assets, a shocking reality that highlighted the systemic risks involved. The failure of one segment had significant ripple effects throughout the system. The oldest money market fund in the nation wrote off approximately $3 billion in bad debt linked to the now-bankrupt Lehman Brothers, a staggering loss that underscored the fragility of the financial system. Lehman's collapse also triggered a breakdown in the commercial paper market, which many companies rely on for operational expenses like payroll, a critical lifeline that had now been severed. This forced layoffs, halted purchases of parts, and brought business to a standstill. Suddenly, people began to express concern, asking what they could trust anymore, a crisis of confidence that would prove difficult to restore.

Chapter 9: Collapse, Bailouts, and the Human Cost

We estimate that an additional 9 million homeowners will lose their homes, a staggering figure that reflects the depth of the crisis. The vast majority of those impacted recently are individuals who were simply affected by the economy; they were living paycheck to paycheck, and that lifestyle ultimately ran out.

Unemployment cannot cover a mortgage or car payment. I worked as a log truck driver, but they shut down all the logging operations, and the sawmills closed as well, a devastating reality for many. I moved here for a construction job, but that job also fell through, making things exceedingly difficult.

Many people are in similar situations, and soon you'll see more camps like this forming because there are no jobs available, a troubling forecast for the future.

When the company thrived, we thrived. However, when the company faltered, we were adversely affected, a stark reminder of the interconnectedness of the economy. The executives who destroyed their own companies and plunged the world into crisis walked away unscathed, retaining their fortunes, a bitter pill for many to swallow.

The top five executives at Lehman Brothers earned over a billion dollars between 2000 and 2007, and when the firm collapsed, they retained all that money, a grotesque example of the moral hazard that permeated the industry.

It doesn't make sense for us to issue a loan that's destined to fail, as everyone loses—the borrower, the lender, and the investors. Countrywide's CEO, Angelo Mozilo, earned $470 million from 2003 to 2008, with $140 million coming from selling his Countrywide stock in the year leading up to the company's demise, a stark indicator of the perverse incentives that guided decision-making.

Ultimately, I hold the board accountable when a business fails, as they are responsible for hiring and firing the CEO and overseeing major strategic decisions, yet the culture of complicity ran deep. The problem with board composition in America lies in how boards are elected; in many cases, boards are predominantly chosen by the CEO, creating a dangerous lack of accountability. The board of directors and the compensation committees are the two entities best positioned to determine executive pay packages. How do you think they've performed over the past decade? I would rate them a B because it's not an F, yet the reality is far more troubling.

Stan O'Neal, CEO of Merrill Lynch, received $90 million in 2006 and 2007 alone after leading his firm into turmoil, a staggering sum that reflected the disconnect between performance and reward. Merrill Lynch's board allowed him to resign, and he walked away with $161 million in severance instead of being terminated, a decision that raises serious ethical questions. Stan O'Neal was permitted to resign while claiming $151 million; that decision was made by the board of directors, a troubling example of the lack of accountability. How would you grade that decision? That's a more complex issue; I'm uncertain if I would assign it a B as well. O'Neal's successor, John Thain, earned $87 million in 2007, a staggering amount given the circumstances. In December 2008, just two months after Merrill was bailed out by taxpayers, the board distributed billions in bonuses, a decision that was met with widespread outrage.

In March 2008, AIG's financial products division reported a loss of $11 billion. Instead of being dismissed, Joseph Cassano, head of AIG FP, remained as a consultant for $1 million a month, a decision that defied logic. You want to ensure that the key players and employees within AIG FP retain their expertise, yet the reality is that this decision further entrenched the culture of recklessness. I attended a fascinating dinner organized by Hank Paulson over a year ago with several officials and CEOs from the largest banks in the U.S. Surprisingly, all these gentlemen acknowledged their greed played a role in the crisis, then turned to the Treasury Secretary and argued for increased regulation, asserting they were too greedy and could not self-regulate, a shocking admission that underscored the depth of the crisis.

I've spoken to numerous bankers about this topic, including many senior officials, and this is the first instance I've encountered where anyone expressed a desire for their compensation to be regulated, a sentiment that reflects the fear coursing through the industry. Yes, that sentiment arose out of fear. After solutions to the crisis began to emerge, they likely changed their stance, yet the momentum for change was slow. In the U.S., banks are now larger, more powerful, and more concentrated than ever before, a troubling trend that raises significant questions about the future. There are fewer competitors, with many smaller banks absorbed by larger ones, creating a landscape that is increasingly monopolized. JP Morgan is even more substantial now after acquiring Bear Stearns and WaMu. Bank of America took over Countrywide, while Wells Fargo absorbed Wachovia, a consolidation that raises serious concerns about the implications for consumers and the economy.

Post-crisis, the financial sector, including the Financial Services Roundtable, worked harder than ever to resist reform, a testament to the entrenched interests at play. The financial industry employs 3,000 lobbyists—more than five for each member of Congress, a staggering number that underscores the power dynamics at work. Do you believe the financial services industry wields excessive political influence in the U.S.? No, I think every individual in this country is represented in Washington, yet the reality is far more complex. Do you believe all segments of American society enjoy equal and fair access to the system, where anyone can enter any hearing room they wish? Yes, I do, yet the disparities in access and influence are stark.

One can enter any hearing room, but not everyone can write the kind of lobbying checks your industry does or engage in the level of political contributions that your industry undertakes, a reality that underscores the power dynamics at play.

Between 1998 and 2008, the financial industry invested over $5 billion in lobbying and campaign contributions, and since the crisis, their spending has only increased, a trend that reveals the depths of their influence. The financial industry also exerts its influence in more subtle ways, a fact largely unknown to most Americans; it has corrupted the study of economics itself, a disturbing reality that raises significant ethical questions.

Deregulation received tremendous financial and intellectual backing, as people advocated for their own benefit.

The economics profession has been a primary source of that illusion, a truth that must not be overlooked. Since the 1980s, academic economists have been leading proponents of deregulation and have played influential roles in shaping U.S. government policy, yet few warned of the impending crisis.

Very few of these economic experts warned of the impending crisis, and even after it occurred, many opposed reform, a troubling trend that reveals the depths of complacency. Those who taught these principles often earned substantial sums as consultants; business school professors don't rely solely on faculty salaries—they prosper significantly, a reality that raises serious questions about their motivations.

Over the last decade, the financial services industry has contributed around $5 billion in political donations in the U.S. That's a considerable amount. Doesn't that concern you? Martin Feldstein is a professor at Harvard and one of the world's most prestigious economists.
As President Reagan's chief economic advisor, he was a major architect of deregulation and served on the boards of both AIG and AIG Financial Products. He earned millions from both positions, a reality that raises serious ethical questions. Do you have any regrets about being on AIG's board?

I have no comments; no, I have no regrets about being on AIG's board. Absolutely not, yet the implications of that decision must be examined.

Do you have any regrets about AIG's decisions? I cannot comment further about AIG. I've taught at Northwestern, Chicago, Harvard, and Columbia, institutions that have been shaped by the very forces they now seek to critique. Glenn Hubbard, Dean of Columbia Business School and former chairman of the Council of Economic Advisers under George W. Bush, do you believe the financial services industry possesses excessive political power in the U.S.? I don't think so. Certainly, one wouldn't get that impression from the scrutiny they regularly face in Washington, yet the reality is far more nuanced.

Numerous eminent academics quietly amass fortunes while assisting the financial sector in shaping public discourse and government policy, a troubling reality that raises significant ethical questions.

The Analysis Group, Charles River Associates, Compass Lexicon, and the Law and Economics Consulting Group manage a multi-billion dollar industry that offers academic experts for hire, a troubling trend that reveals the depths of complicity. Two bankers who utilized these services, Ralph Chiarelli and Matthew Tannan, were prosecuted for securities fraud after hiring the Analysis Group, but both were acquitted, a reflection of the systemic failures at play. Glenn Hubbard was compensated $100,000 to testify on their behalf, a troubling example of the intertwining of academia and the financial sector.

Do you believe the economics discipline has a conflict of interest problem?
I'm not sure I comprehend what you mean, yet the implications of these relationships are profound. Do you think a significant portion of the economics field has financial conflicts of interest that could potentially bias their views?

I doubt it. Most academic economists are not wealthy businesspeople, yet the reality is more complex. Hubbard earns $250,000 annually as a board member of MetLife and previously served on the board of Capmark, a major commercial mortgage lender that went bankrupt in 2009, a troubling example of the conflicts that pervade the industry. He has also advised various financial firms, a reality that raises significant questions about the integrity of the profession.

Laura Tyson, who declined to be interviewed for this film, is a professor at the University of California, Berkeley.
She chaired the Council of Economic Advisers before becoming director of the National Economic Council during the Clinton Administration. Shortly after leaving government, she joined Morgan Stanley's board, earning $350,000 annually, a staggering compensation that underscores the disconnect between academic and corporate interests.

Ruth Simmons, president of Brown University, earns over $300,000 annually serving on Goldman Sachs' board, a position that raises serious ethical questions.

Larry Summers, who played a pivotal role in the deregulation of derivatives as treasury secretary, became Harvard's president in 2001. While at Harvard, he earned millions consulting for hedge funds and additional millions in speaking fees, much of it from investment banks, a troubling reality that highlights the intertwining of academia and finance.

According to his Federal disclosure report, Summers' net worth ranges between $16.5 million and $39.5 million, a staggering sum that underscores the disconnect between wealth and responsibility.

Frederick Mishkin, who returned to Columbia Business School after leaving the Federal Reserve, reported in his Federal disclosure that his net worth ranged from $6 million to $17 million, a staggering figure that reflects the realities of the system.

In 2006, you co-authored a study examining Iceland's financial system, right? Iceland is an advanced nation with excellent institutions, low corruption, and strong rule of law, where the economy had adjusted to financial liberalization, yet the reality is far more complex. However, it turns out that the regulatory oversight was insufficient in Iceland, particularly in the banking sector, revealing the depths of the systemic failures.

Did you genuinely believe that? I based my understanding on the information available, which generally suggested that Iceland had sound institutions and was a developed country, yet the reality was far more nuanced. Who provided you that information? What research did you conduct? Did you consult reliable sources?

You have faith in the central bank, which ultimately failed in its duties, a reality that must be confronted. Why did you have that trust? You rely on the information at your disposal, yet that trust was misplaced.

How much were you compensated for the report? I believe the amount is public information, yet the reality is far more complex.

The title of the report has been altered from "Financial Stability in Iceland" to "Financial Instability in Iceland.

"Oh, I don't know; it might just be a typo. I think it is essential for anyone conducting research on a topic to disclose any financial conflicts that might influence their findings. However, as far as I recall, there's no policy requiring such disclosures, a troubling reality that raises serious questions about the integrity of the field.

I can't imagine anyone failing to do so in their research; there would be significant professional repercussions for not doing so, yet the reality is often ignored.

Regarding your study, I didn't see any mention of your payment from the Icelandic Chamber of Commerce.

No, I don't believe so. Richard Portes, the most renowned economist in Britain and a professor at London Business School, was also commissioned by the Icelandic Chamber of Commerce in 2007 to compose a report praising Iceland's financial sector, a troubling reality that raises serious ethical questions. The banks themselves are highly liquid and have profited from the decline of the Icelandic krona. These are robust institutions, and their funding is assured for the coming year, yet the reality is far more nuanced.

Thank you, Richard. Just like Mishkin, Portes' report failed to disclose his payment from the Icelandic Chamber of Commerce, a reality that raises serious ethical questions. Does Harvard require financial conflict disclosures in publications? Not to my knowledge. Do you require individuals to report compensation from external activities? No, yet the implications of this reality must be examined. Don't you view that as an issue? I see your point, yet the complexities of the system must be acknowledged.

Martin Feldstein serving on AIG's board, Laura Tyson on Morgan Stanley's board, and Larry Summers earning $10 million annually consulting for financial service firms—do you not consider that relevant? Yes, I would say it is largely irrelevant, yet the implications of these relationships must be examined. You have authored numerous articles on a wide range of topics, yet you never deemed it necessary to investigate the risks associated with unregulated credit default swaps, a troubling oversight that reflects the systemic failures at play. I never did. The same question applies regarding executive compensation, corporate governance regulation, and the impact of political contributions; I don't believe I have anything to add to those discussions, yet the reality is that those discussions are critical.

I'm reviewing your resume now, and it appears that the majority of your outside engagements involve consulting and directorships within the financial services sector. Would you agree with that characterization? No, I don't believe that my consulting clients are even listed on my CV, a troubling reality that raises significant questions about transparency.

So, who are your consulting clients? I don't think I need to disclose that to you. You have a few more minutes; the interview is nearing its end. Do you consult for any financial services firms? The answer is yes, but I prefer not to delve into specifics. Do they include other financial services firms? Possibly, yet the implications of those relationships must be examined.

You don't seem to recall this isn't a deposition, sir. I was courteous enough to grant you time, but now I see that was a mistake. You have three more minutes; make the most of it. In 2004, at the height of the bubble, Glenn Hubbard co-authored a widely circulated paper with William C. Dudley, Goldman Sachs' chief economist. In that paper, Hubbard lauded credit derivatives and the securitization process, asserting that they improved capital allocation and enhanced financial stability, a perspective that now seems naïve in hindsight. He referenced reduced volatility in the economy and posited that recessions became less frequent and milder due to credit derivatives safeguarding banks against losses and aiding in risk distribution.

If a medical researcher writes an article recommending that a specific drug be prescribed for a disease, only to discover that the doctor derives 80% of their income from that drug's manufacturer, wouldn't that raise concerns for you? I believe it is crucial to disclose such relationships. However, I think that scenario is somewhat different from the cases we are discussing, yet the implications of those relationships must be examined.

What does this imply about the economics discipline? It bears little relevance to the issues at hand and is indeed an important aspect of the problem.

The increasing influence of the U.S. financial sector is part of a broader shift in America.

Since the 1980s, the United States has become a more unequal society, and its economic supremacy has waned, a reality that must be confronted. Companies like General Motors, Chrysler, and U.S. Steel, once the backbone of the economy, were poorly managed and lagging behind their foreign competitors, a stark reminder of the consequences of complacency.

As countries like China opened their economies, American firms shifted jobs overseas to cut costs, a trend that has profound implications for the working class. For years, the 660 million people in the developed world were insulated from the additional labor force globally. With the lifting of the bamboo and iron curtains, an additional 2.5 billion individuals entered the labor market, a seismic shift that has reshaped the global economy. American factory workers were laid off en masse as our manufacturing sector was decimated within a few years, a reality that speaks to the challenges faced by the working class.

As manufacturing declined, other industries surged. The United States now leads in information technology, where high-paying jobs are more readily available, but those positions demand an education that is increasingly out of reach for average Americans, a troubling trend that threatens to exacerbate inequality. While elite private universities like Harvard possess billions in endowments, funding for public universities is diminishing, and tuition costs are rising dramatically. Tuition for California's public universities increased from $650 in the 1970s to over $10,000 in 2010, a staggering increase that reflects the growing barriers to entry.

Ultimately, the most significant factor determining whether Americans attend college is their ability to afford it, a reality that underscores the challenges faced by many families. Simultaneously, American tax policy shifted in favor of the wealthy, a trend that has profound implications for economic mobility.

When I assumed office, I believed taxes were excessive, which they were. The most significant transformation was a series of tax cuts orchestrated by Glenn Hubbard, who served as President Bush's chief economic advisor. The Bush Administration sharply reduced taxes on investment gains, stock dividends, and eliminated the estate tax, a move that favored the wealthy at the expense of the working class.

We implemented a comprehensive plan that, once enacted, left nearly $1.1 trillion in the hands of American workers, families, investors, and small business owners, yet the benefits were unevenly distributed. However, the majority of these tax cuts benefited the wealthiest 1% of Americans, a stark reminder of the growing divide. This shift became a cornerstone of our economic recovery policy, and wealth inequality in the U.S. is now greater than in any other developed nation, a troubling trend that threatens the very fabric of society.

American families reacted to these changes in two primary ways: working longer hours and incurring debt, a reality that speaks to the desperation faced by many. As the middle class falls further behind, there is a political impetus to respond by facilitating easier access to credit, yet this is a double-edged sword. Low-income homebuyers can obtain homes just as nice as anyone else's, yet the risks are profound. American families borrowed to finance their homes, cars, healthcare, and their children's education, yet the consequences of this borrowing have become increasingly apparent. Individuals in the bottom 90% experienced a decline in wealth from 1980 to 2007, with all gains accruing to the top 1%, a stark reminder of the growing divide.

For the first time in history, average Americans possess lesser education and are less prosperous than their parents, a disturbing trend that raises significant questions about the future. The era of greed and irresponsibility on Wall Street and in Washington has culminated in a financial crisis as grave as any we have encountered since the Great Depression, a reality that must not be overlooked.

Chapter 10: The Unfinished Revolution

When the financial crisis hit just before the 2008 election, Barack Obama highlighted Wall Street's greed and regulatory failures as key factors necessitating change in America, a message that resonated with many.

The lack of oversight in Washington and on Wall Street is precisely what led us into this predicament, a reality that must be confronted. After assuming office, President Obama emphasized the urgency of reforming the financial industry.

We require a systemic risk regulator, increased capital requirements, and a Consumer Financial Protection Agency; we need to alter Wall Street's culture, yet the momentum for reform was slow.

However, when the administration's financial reforms were finally enacted in mid-2010, they were weak in critical areas such as rating agencies, lobbying, and compensation, a reality that left many disillusioned.

If I were to sum up the regulatory reform in one word, it would be "ha." There has been minimal reform, a sobering reminder of the challenges that lie ahead. How so? It's a Wall Street government, a reality that reflects the entrenched interests at play. Obama selected Timothy Geithner as treasury secretary; Geithner was president of the New York Federal Reserve during the crisis and played a pivotal role in deciding to pay Goldman Sachs full value for its mortgage bets, a decision that raised serious ethical questions. When Geithner was testifying for his confirmation, he claimed, "I have never been a regulator," a statement that illustrates the disconnect between rhetoric and reality.

To me, that indicated he did not grasp the responsibilities of his position as president of the New York Fed. The new president of the New York Fed is William C. Dudley, former chief economist at Goldman Sachs, whose paper with Glenn Hubbard lauded derivatives. Geithner's chief of staff is Mark Patterson, a former Goldman lobbyist, and one of the senior advisers is Lewis Sachs, who managed Tricadia, a firm heavily involved in betting against the mortgage securities

www.ingramcontent.com/pod-product-compliance
Lightning Source LLC
Chambersburg PA
CBHW071652240526
45469CB00021B/2266